From The Depth Of My Soul

AF624586

Janet Erlam

BookLeaf Publishing

Presentation by *BookLeaf Publishing*

Web: www.bookleafpub.com

E-mail: info@bookleafpub.com

ISBN: 9789357212113

First edition 2023

DEDICATION

To God first, without whom I would not have survived.

To my beautiful daughter and world Gillian, my greatest achievement and her brother Andrew, who waits in eternity.

And my grandson, who showed me there was adventure in dreams.

ACKNOWLEDGEMENT

To my daughter Gillian who has stood with me always; my fellow companion in so much darkness, both fighting the legacy of someone we loved so dearly.

To Andrew my son and the Borchardt warriors who inspire so much, in his memory and always with love.

To my grandson, named for his uncle, Andrew my second chance.

My son in law Ian.

My family, now in eternity, who were always there.

To God who gives me the words, who never left me, even when I left him.

And all those who I cherish as friends, Denise, Anna, Carole, Paula and Maureen. Years have been spent always bonded.

PREFACE

Once upon a time, on a child's cancer and leukaemia ward, a kind of hopeless place, filled with vast amounts of bravery as knights and princesses fought for survival, I found a tiny scrap of pink paper.

My son had been drawing, he was asleep and I was in tears, not knowing how long he would be mine to hold.

I had long loved paper and pen, unlike today, I had no abundance of stationery, so I picked up my pen, said a prayer, listened and began to write. I opened the door to what would become my salvation. To express but to listen to God.

Fairy tales are dark but filled with bravery and inspiration and that was where I was. The ward faded and all these little characters rose up to inspire. Brave little characters that fought until there was nothing left but to adventure on, into eternity.

I was left with the memories and the words that fill me heart and soul, my faith was broken but the inspiration of my toddler son would lead me to greater faith and greater words but most of all, greater love.

Savage Tango

Eyes across the dance floor; it happens every time,
Pulsating rhythm to hypnotise, this is just a sign.
Pulled to body contact, mesmerised by fate,
Feeling the heat to snap and flick, feet don't want to wait.
It's the same all the time, this dance that calls of love,
Yet I know body and soul, this is only lust.
Your eyes don't speak of wonder, just a savage dance,
I am led continuously, caught up in this trance.
You smoulder and you burn the passion blazes high,
Yet all will be in ashes, dampened by the tears I cry.
There is nothing real or soulful, just a moment nothing more.
This is it and there will never be, another rousing encore.
It's a dance and connection, perfection in bodies entwined,
But the love I feel inside for you, doesn't mean I'm blind.
I can't make you love me and you don't, and when love's the golden rule,

I fall short within this tango, I'm just a dancing fool.
The savage way you hold me, leaves me truly in no doubt.
That I am nothing in your eyes, for you don't know what love's about.

Pink Paper

The bleeps and cries, the harrowed sounds,
You asleep at peace.
I just sit in silence,
With prayers that never cease.
A piece of scrap pink paper,
That is left from what you drew.
I sit, I think, I formulate.
What I think of you.
Love that now seems to lead to heartbreak,
Prayers not answered the way I see,
How long do we have left my son?
How long is you and me?
Upon the paper before me,
My words unfold with tears.
I really thought we had a life,
Not a couple of years.
The voice of the Creator,
Cultivates my darkest thoughts,
I pour out from the depth of me,
Deep within my protected fort.
The words become my outpouring,
The voice within my soul.
My expression of the unthinkable,
A prayer to make me whole.
A tiny piece of paper,

That was to become the key.
To voice the way I truly feel,
Long after you left me.

The Girl In The Suitcase

High on the wardrobe, it has sat so long,
Far beyond my tears.
Inside, the girl preserved and kept,
Through long and lonely years.
I think of her now, the giggles and smiles,
The hope and fairy-tale ending.
When life was sweet and there were no holes,
That clearly needed mending.
I know she's there but I won't peek,
I'm ashamed of what she'll see.
For I am but a shadow now,
Of what she used to be.
Before cruelty and all the pain,
Before Innocence was lost.
Then I became the creature that,
Bore a heavy cross.
The laughter gone, the tears that fell,
The heart that broke in two.
The girl in the suitcase protected thus,
Could quite easily be you.
I miss her and her laughing eyes,
The skip within her step.
I wonder if she saw me now,
Would she remember, when we met.
It feels so distant, long-lost shore,

Another realm, another time.
And I feel tarnished by the pain,
As I long for what was mine.

A Crisis of Faith

Dear Lord, I didn't mean it literally,
When I prayed that prayer.
Lord were you mistaken,
When you sent me there?
Lord, I didn't want it to be my child,
The child that had to die.
I only asked you to send me to help,
Not to make me cry.

Lord, I want to go now,
I cannot think to stay.
Lord, I don't want to praise you,
When my child has gone away.
I'm in pain and I'm in anguish,
It was not what my faith implied.
I thought you answered prayer Lord,
Instead, I sat and cried.

I am walking out of here Lord,
You do not need to come.
I'm a leper and an outcast,
A mum without her son.
His little light was a beacon,
In a world that needed him.
I'm left to walk in darkness, now,

You made that small light dim.

Honestly Lord, I'm being truthful,
The pain burns, so I won't lie.
Why didn't you say my walk with you?
Would simply make me cry.
No Lord, I'm not listening,
Why me, Lord, why send me?
How can I help another?
When it's so hard to be free?

So, all the time I ran,
A little beacon from the heaven's glowed.
My child was like a lighthouse,
Pointed at the Lord.
He directioned me to Calvary,
And there upon the Cross.
I realised where God had sent me,
Because like me, he's suffered loss.

Forever Young

Humanity did its worst, and you are forever gold,
You are the heartbreak story; you will not grow old.
I lost the laughter that rang in these walls, yet the world still turns,
You never left the heart of me, and my love for you, still burns.
I see your face encased in glass, my fingers cannot touch,
Forever young, I miss your smile, the hands I cannot clutch.
I call your name when I awake, and not a day goes by,
That you aren't in my heart and soul, still my eyes can cry.
When I realise how much I love you, that I cannot hold your hand,
Time never made a difference; I still don't understand.
Forever gold the memories, a soul beautiful and free,
The sun still shines, the moon still glows and forever that will be.

Your wisdom was beyond all this, transcending time and space,
You were meant for heavenly things beyond the human race.
Your smile still brightens up my walls, your faith it fills my soul,
Forever young as time ticks on, grief can take its toll.

Salvation

The dark spirit and council of the night arose,
The shadows whispered lies.
Judgement on actions that made me black,
Ugly in their eyes.

I stood before them condemned by shame,
When the Spirit of light arose.
He had been quenched, resisted and grieved,
When my heart in ice, had froze.

"Who is this advocate?" the darkness boomed,
"I am the paraclete of love," he said.
The darkness laughed, "you've come for this?
Whose love is long since dead."

I stood in shame, my burden heavy,
Convicted by my darkest deed.
The breath of the Almighty stood,
Ready to intercede.

I represent experientially,
Having been tempted yet without sin.
I see the heart to know the deed,
I know what lies within.

I know the torment and the pain,
The distraction from the path.
The frozen heart in fragile state.
The inability to laugh.

I plead only before the righteous judge,
Be gone now with your fear.
I am personal and permanent,
Be gone, you have no jurisdiction here.

Night

When darkness falls and neon flashes,
Upon the city streets.
It's a time when faded lovers,
In the cold night air can meet,
Likened souls like vampires,
Who cannot greet the sun.
Only moonlight's silver rays,
Helps them do, what must be done.
Where broken hearts lie wasted,
Where a need has to be met.
Where nothing is forever,
And tonight is all you get.
So many wander freely,
Just to scratch an itch.
For love is long forgotten,
And life is such a bitch.
It's safer in the shadows,
The scars don't look the same.
Like calls to like, they tell me,
No one cares about a name.
This is where the broken go,
Minds numbed and hearts in pieces.
Where music thrums and souls are lost,
Where for a minute, all hurt ceases.
But night gives way to daylight,

And once more reality bites.
They would be doing better,
If it wasn’t for the nights.

The Sound Of A Breaking Heart

So silently it shatters, cracks formulate and snap,
No one hears a heart break, intuition often lacked.
Nothingness is what is seen, a smile to hide the tears,
Silence, no words spoken, amidst the hidden fears.
That should the truth be told, or perceived, a leper you would be,
Treated with disdain, where shame is all you see.
Rejection and indifference, control the shattered state.
Yet no one knows the story of what causes a heart to break.
The incognito stance to cover up the pain,
A smile to create sunshine, when walking in the rain.
For how can you vocalise, the trauma that you feel?
How can you talk about it, when talking makes it real?
The sound of a breaking heart is a lonely, invisible way,
A person all alone, who could not get love to stay.

Raven

The damp swirling ground mists, obscure my feet from view,
Yet I am sure footed, educated by darkness too.
The skeletal trees that do not bend or break, are surely just like me.
Shadows hide my form and I feel quite safe you see.
A shallow, silvery light, that blinks so way up high.
That calls to me in soothing tones, begging me to fly.
I cannot come, I will not scale, the pinnacles and heights,
For I'm a creature darkness forged, not akin to heights.
Night-time is my playground; shadows are my kin.
Hindered by the broken heart, that I still feel within.
And though the soft moon calls my name, I speak only from a shadowed haven.
No beauty, no light, can cling to me; I am the darkest raven.
"Come to me," the silver light begs, "Come dance with me, be free.

Come bathe in moonlight, soak your soul,
dearest raven, come and see.

Unrequited

I wanted to be the princess, the one he would battle for,
But he sees me as a friend, an ally.
There are no silver words from his lips,
No honey dripping through his tones.
For I am not the kind of love he would aspire to battle dragons for,
Maybe a trusty side kick, someone to share confidences.
But there is nothing here to win his heart,
Nothing here to capture that look that rises deep from the soul.
Though we laugh together,
I am not that girl he would crave,
The one his eyes alight upon and sensuality erupts,
Like a volcano of passion and longing.
I content myself with his nearness, I hide my feelings,
Deep in the pits of my own soul.
When the moon rises, I walk silently, sharing my secrets,
The moon knows how I feel. The stars are my confidants,
And night-time hides my expressions of love.

To protect me from the rejection should he ever,
Know my heart.

Transformation

From a tiny rivulet deep in the mountains,
The water flows with momentum.
Happily tripping along the rivulet,
Becomes a stream gaining strength.
It is no longer a trickle,
It becomes a babbling brook, ever flowing.
The flow cannot return to where it originated,
It is learning and growing, ever forward,
Into a mighty river.
It is no longer a babbling brook.
Then a mighty ocean awaits, calling, welcoming.
But the river must take a risk, it cannot flow backwards,
Does the river fear?
No, it goes onwards and becomes one, with the ocean,
With the vast expanse of water, it is absorbed into a whole,
Mightier than it ever was.
It is no longer a river.
By overcoming fear, we become mightier,
We learn from the trials and tribulations.
It is not about being absorbed,
It is about becoming.
It is about transformation into a mighty expanse,
Only, then, to know true potential.

Goodbye Again

She repacks her bag, she has been here before,
Neatly layers her life and heads out of the door.
No need now to look back, her pride must be intact.
No need to blame herself, it was something that he lacked.

No happy ever after, does it even exist?
What is the time limit on a lovers kiss?
Nothing is forever, nothing stays the same,
Start out on a sunlit path, end it in the rain.

She will mourn and she will grieve, she will rise again,
This will be another segment, of 'remember when?'
She will gather up her best bits, she will smile once more,
She will take all she has learned and add it to her treasure store.

For now a door is closing but hope will not be lost,
Just another avenue, for her to to take her cross.
Faith will be the fuel that keeps her hope alive,

That she will find the one true love, to help her to survive.

Age Is Just A Number

In a dusty corner of the attic, sits an old trunk.
She is in there, the girl I look for.
A girl hidden away in yesterday,
The one who loved music, loved to dance.
Opening the lid, I dare to take a peek,
She sits, no longer expectant,
Her dancing shoes beside her.
She wants to dance some more,
But life beat her down, as the glow died down,
Lines on her face, pain in her bones,
Deeming her past her prime and she listened,
Until today.
The feet that danced want to dance still,
The music in her soul is alive and vibrant.
Indulging her inner teen, she allows her
freedom,
To dance again.
Too old is not an option,
When your spirit dances and sings,
Age is just a number.

Hope For Eternity

High on a hill, as the thunder cracked,
And lightening tore at the sky.
A scene unfolded and met my eyes,
And yet I wondered why.
That day bogged down in sorrow,
Filled with sin and shame,
I set out on a quest for hope,
A way to clear my name.
Long I sought frivolity,
Long my eyes distracted.
Caught up in a web of lies,
And sin, that I'd attracted.
I saw him then upon the cross,
His eyes were fixed on me,
I knew he was my only hope,
Yet how could this truly be?
Beside him hung two thieves,
One called out to him.
He told the man he would saved,
Amidst the thunder's din.
Hie eyes held such forgiveness,
In a body beaten and bruised.
The sin of the world hung on him,
What had I to lose?
I stood beneath a cruel cross,

I believed and did repent.
He closed his eyes and died for me,
This was the reason he was sent.

Poem

A poem should be a thing of wonder,
Words inspired within the soul.
That speaks clearly and concisely,
For people as a whole.
No one should be discriminated against,
By terms that make so sense.
Appellation should be simple,
To understand,
What is clearly meant.
The basic elements of language,
Given simply to express.
Not convoluted sentences,
That inspire people just to guess.
Where nothing makes much sense,
But like the Emperors new clothes,
People pretend to understand,
When really no one knows.
The reader needs to be drawn in,
To feel the soul's delight.
To bathe within a sentence,
Seeing beyond sight.
No one should be excluded,
From this beauty of painted words.
Simplicity, rhyming and beauty,
Not confusion written by nerds.

Childhood

Dreams and wonder, sweet delight.
Eyes that hungrily seek.
Games and laughter, carefree spirits,
Learning the ability to speak.
Fairy tales and secret woods,
Adventure and mystery too.
Where worries have no lease,
And of darkness, there is no clue.
Where songs rise cheerily and laughter flows,
Like a tiny babbling brook.
Where stories lie on every page,
Of an exciting picture book.
Those carefree days that make us smile,
When love brings a balmy haze.
Oh how soon they are over,
Those innocent childhood days.
For when we grow and darkness looms,
It's easy to wish we were back in those days.
To feel the security we procured,
In those sweet, pleasant and simple, pathways.

Childhood Spent

How long I sat in awesome wonder,
Listening to stories of what love would bring.
Childlike visions filled my soul,
Of my prince who would, one day, bear a ring.
Music and joy; fairy tale pictures,
I waited with longing for that day.
Until he came and caught my heart,
And took my childhood, clean away.
Blinded by his love filled passion,
Words of love so quickly fell.
Believing I was besotted, easily taken,
Until my world was turned to hell.
The pretty colours shrouded a savage tunic,
Pretty words, covered a million lies.
Words of love, to disguise the lust,
Horror that slowly opened my eyes.
No fairy tale, just pure heartbreak,
The ravishing that stole my treasure.
No handsome prince, just a narcissistic lover,
Who raped the promise of forever.
Childhood spent, dreams in tatters,
No fair heroine, just a lonely soul.
Who once believed in love's first kiss,
And no longer, has a treasured goal.

Horizon

I stand upon a granite headland,
Storm clouds threaten, billows roll.
Sea mist rises, obscuring vision,
The worn down conflict of my soul.
I wait and wonder subdued by loss,
Yet across the distant shore.
Through the mist a far horizon,
A boat sets sail for distant shores.
The sea waves crash, the boat is hardy,
Moving forward, I watch it go.
Smaller and smaller, grows the vessel,
As it aims for that distant shore.
Over there, others are waiting,
Sending up a joyful sound.
Awaiting the passengers on that vessel,
Coming home where love is found.
And so I see that those I love,
Now alight on a distant beach.
Greeted warmly, with love and singing,
As other arms, for their bodies reach.
So I, in sadness, feel the hope,
From the horizon far and wide.
A goodbye here is a hello waiting,
From loved ones, on the other side.

Indifference

A shadow passing by, weaving along the crowded street,
Unobtrusive by design, not someone you wish to meet.
Happy people passing by, laughter in the air,
Passing by unnoticed, no one seems to care.
The lonely and the broken hearted that no one ever sees,
Far too wrapped up in trivial things, in a selfish world of me.
Invisible in a world of self, where looks are scrutinised,
Where no one observes a nomad, that doesn't register in their eyes.
Mankind has grown more cruel, but subtle in its ways,
Indifference is a weapon, oh what a part that plays.
For mankind chooses to ignore, what doesn't fit the mould,
Looking down its nose, eyes are hard and an attitude that's cold.
Passing by they leave him; a silent figure in the rain,

They do not sense his mercy, know nothing of his pain.
They know nothing of his sacrifice, the cross upon a hill,
Know nothing of salvation, this is a bitter pill.
He watches as they pass on by, missing the blessings he wants to bestow,
He senses their mentality; as he watches cruelty soar.
Golgotha now forgotten; Calvary ignored,
Men look at trivialities and very soon are bored.
Human flesh is cheap it seems, love abandoned, greed will rise,
For man ignores the son of God, ignores the tears he cries.
Only the faithful few, who are willing to believe,
Turn their souls, to God above and finally learn to breathe.

Narrative

Cosy nights by the fire's glow,
Snow lay thick and deep.
The crackle of the logs and coal,
Warmth from blazing heat.
Time to take a book and sit,
Quietly to escape.
Into real adventure,
What would be your fate?
Oh those days so imprecise,
Simply didn't matter.
When you simply read a narrative,
And truth really was merely the latter.
Carried along on imagination's wings,
Lost for hours on end.
Caught up with characters and plots,
Wanting broken hearts to mend.
Today computers ruin such,
Graphics violent and obscene.
Children's imagination dies,
Do they know what that word means?
The world of play and reading gone,
No cosy fire to boot.
No storybook heroes to catch up with,
No treasure hunt for loot.
Oh the magic of a physical book,

And still on winter's nights.
I take up a volume, settle down,
Let my imagination take flight.
Far away from a nasty world,
From bullies and selfish things.
I ride with heroes once again,
What magic this all brings.

Leaving

Morning; it's just another day,
Today I know, I will be on my way.
My heart has no home, so I must leave,
The rising sun has no reprieve.
Because I cannot put into your heart,
The love that needs a seed to start.
For me it's real, I lay down arms,
Give up on this fight, I have no charm.
Though I tried with all my might
I know I will be alone tonight.
Unrequited love; the endless pain,
Starting out on this road again.
I cannot stay where no feeling stirs,
Where love is absent, you don't care.
Don't patronise me, let me go,
Let me find what I need to know.
Out there I may just find the one,
And you can simply carry on.
I lay down my heart and turn away,
Baggage in hand, into a new day.
Tears in my eyes, I know just what to do,
Because you don't love me, the way I love you.

www.ingramcontent.com/pod-product-compliance
Lightning Source LLC
Chambersburg PA
CBHW051746130826
49812CB00033B/1023
9789357212113